MW00885439

SIMON AND THE SOLAR SYSTEM

Copyright © 2017 by Derek Taylor Kent

www.DerekTaylorKent.com

All rights reserved.

Cover art and illustrations by Mary Gutfleisch

No part of this book may be used or reproduced in any manner whatsoever without written permission except in the case of brief quotations embodied in critical articles and reviews.

For information address www.DerekTaylorKent.com

ASIN: B004R1QFT8
ISBN-13: 978-1453898925
ISBN-10: 1453898921

Printed in China

Young Simon Beck lay awake in his bed,
With visions of planets at play in his head.
But Simon was scared; he had no time to rest! For tomorrow was Simon's **ASTRONOMY TEST!**
He'd studied all night, but the facts had not stuck. Was the sun very small or as big as a truck?
Yes, passing this test would require some luck.
THE UNIVERSE

The stars were his passion,
but names weren't enough.
The science behind them –
now that part was tough.

He read in his bed,
but he soon fell asleep,

When something awoke him
that made his heart leap!

A beam from a starlight
streamed into his room!
And something was riding it!
Just like a flume!

The windows burst open
and then with a flash,
A spaceship zoomed in
with no clamor or crash!

It hovered and covered
but most of the floor.
It looked like a speedboat
that traveled onshore.

A hatch opened up
and a creature appeared.
It wore an orange spacesuit,
green skin, and a beard.

"My name is Neil Newton,"
the creature remarked.
"I hope you don't mind
where my spaceship is parked."

"No," said young Simon,
"I certainly don't,
But that doesn't mean that
my parents still won't!"

"Don't worry," said Neil,
"with my 'Time-Warp' device,
Time has now stopped just for us,
ain't that nice?

I'm here on a mission
to give you a tour –
To show you the wonders
of space's grandeur."

"In that little spacecraft?"
said Simon so keen,
"What could I see
that I have not yet seen?"

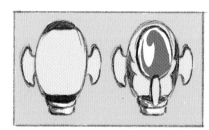

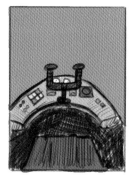

"A lot!" said Neil Newton.

"This ship is a Zoozer!
It's quite a bit better
than everyday cruisers.

We'll zoom in the Zoozer
right through Saturn's rings!
For the Zoozer's a spacecraft
that's built for such things.

The cosmos invites you
tonight as its guest
To see why astronomers'
lives are the best!

From planet to planet
we'll wander with zest
And tomorrow I think
you will ace that old test."

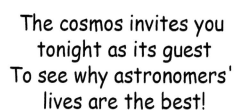

Though normally Simon would not ride with strangers, Something inside him dismissed all the dangers.
They jumped in the Zoozer and buckled their belts
And zoomed into space,
where discoveries dwelt.

Magnetic North Pole
They soared up to space like a sky-cutting blade! Their velocity SMASHING the speed barricade.
Simon gazed upon Earth like a heavenly bird. The vision he saw is not worthy of words!
Detached from this object, this mystical orb, This holder of life with unlimited cords,
He realized that living is life's own reward.
Magnetic South Pole
"Dazzling!" said Newton. "It's like Mona Lisa!
Your planet leans back like the Tower of Pisa!
The tilt of the Earth, at its certain degrees, Causes Sydney to burn while in London they freeze!
The north and south hemisphere alter in season. The angle of sunlight I hear is the reason."

"And look at the planets
and all of the stars!
There's Saturn
and Neptune
and Venus
and Mars!
The rest of the stars
are a distance so vast,
Their light may take eons
to reach us at last!
When you look at a star
you are viewing the past!
To start off the tour
you just think of a spot,
And the Zoozer will trot
to the spot you have thought!
But stay in this system,
that is the one rule.
If you go any further,
we'll run out of fuel."

So Simon thought hard of a good place to spring,
Then found himself flying right through Saturn's rings!
"Oops!" said Neil Newton. "What bad navigation! This ship has been set onto teleportation!
These rings are composed of immense blocks of ice!
If we were to hit one it...
would not be nice."

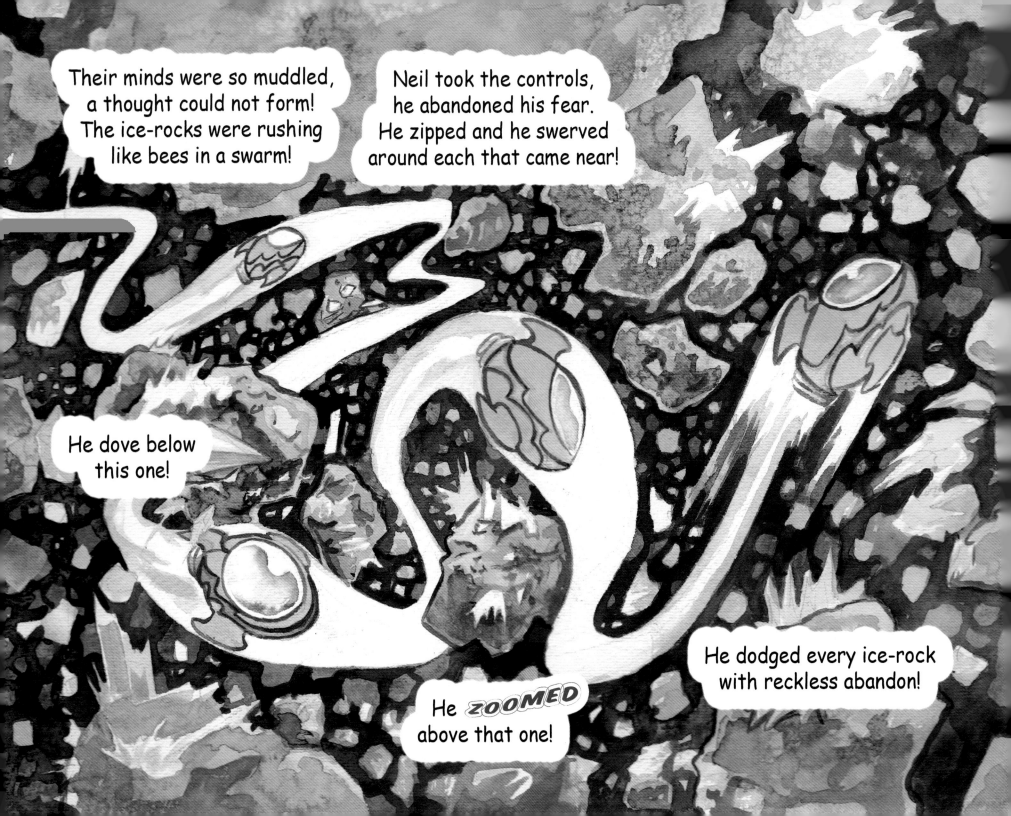

"Although this new order is not as I've planned-it, Let's go on a tour of the gaseous planets.
The gaseous planets are made of thick air, An ocean of gasses that swirl everywhere!
First we see Jupiter, red as an apple,
Where poisonous liquids and gasses wage battle!
Enormous in size, it obscures little Earth -
More than 300 times in celestial girth!
And there at the heart is the giant "Red Spot,"
A storm that has lasted for eons... a lot!
Red Spot
You once were too far, but now look where you are!
Observing a mass that was almost a star!"

"A process called 'fusion'
takes place in its core,
As hydrogen atoms
collide in a war!

This chemical crashing
induces a bond:
New helium's made
and the hydrogen's gone!

By use of this method
it generates heat,
Which supports life on Earth,
and grows plants that we eat."

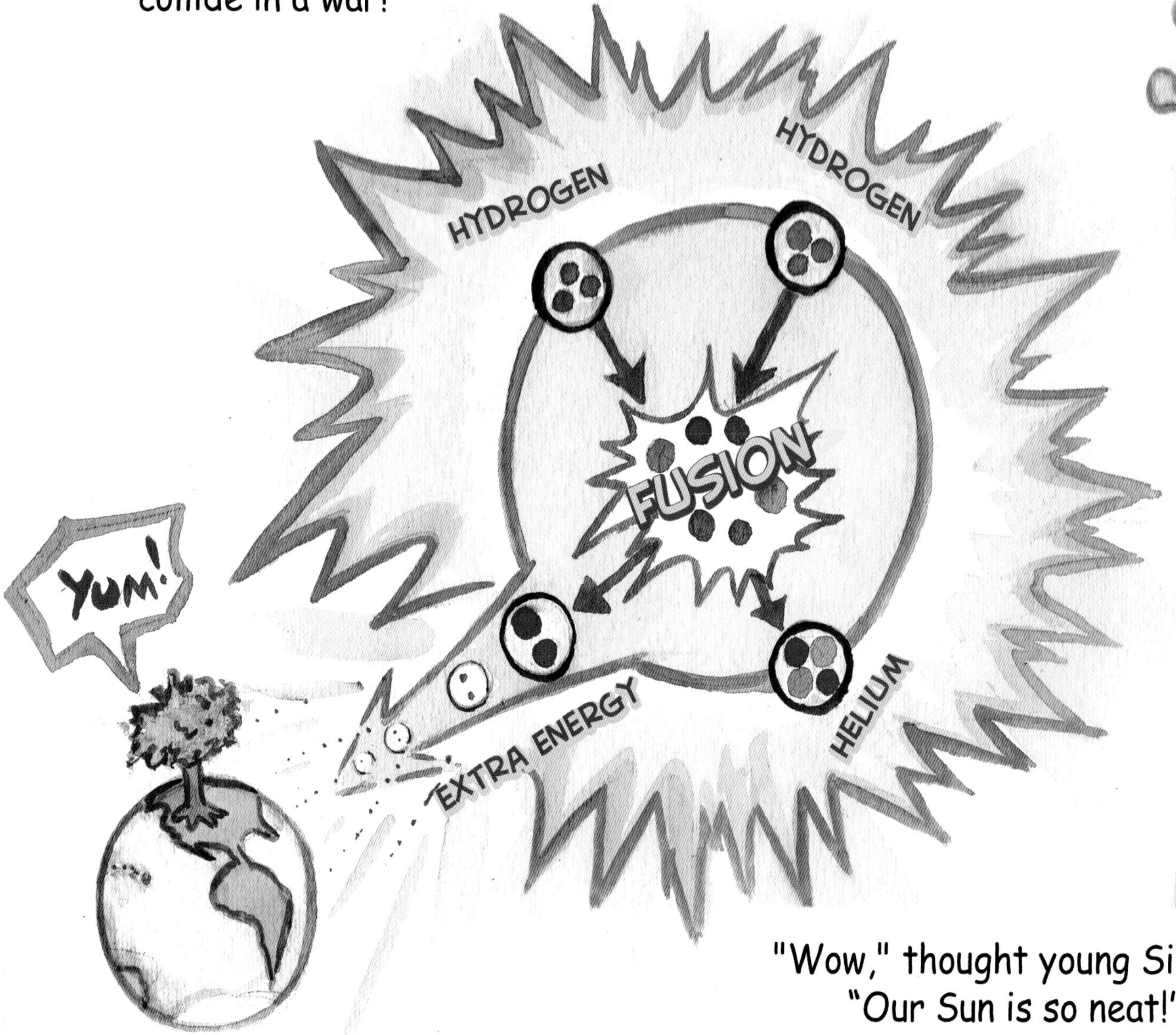

"Wow," thought young Simon.
"Our Sun is so neat!"

"Now buckle your belt
and grab hold of your hair.
My sensors are sensing
a great solar flare!

The magnetic energy
stored in the Sun
Will break free from its chains
and shoot forth like a gun!"

Then just like Neil said,
the hot plasma, once pinned,
ERUPTED! Creating
a great solar wind!

Like riding a wave
to a far distant shore,

They rode the flare home

to the small window door.

"All right," said Neil Newton,
"the tour is complete,

And we barely survived
by the skin of our feet.

We had a good time,
but it's time that we parted,

And speaking of time,

it is time that time started!"

Neil re-pushed the very first button
he pressed,
And time resumed back
from the moment they left.

Neil jumped in the Zoozer
and cried out with zest:

"Goodbye Simon Beck
and good luck on your test!"

The next day at school,
Simon hardly could wait.

He wanted that test
'cause he knew he'd do
great!

But then Mrs. Fiddlebone
mentioned with sorrow:
"I've chosen to postpone
the test till tomorrow."